Wise Publications
London/New York/Sydney

"How Great Thou Art"

Exclusive Distributors:
Music Sales Limited,
8/9 Frith Street,
London W1V 5TZ.
Music Sales Pty Limited,
27 Clarendon Street,
Artarmon, Sydney,
Australia 2064.

"How Great Thou Art"

Cover painting by the studio of David,
reproduced by permission of the National Gallery.

Book designed by Pearce Marchbank.

This book © Copyright 1976 and 1986 by Wise Publications
ISBN 0.7119.0808.7
AM 61706

"Rock Of Ages"

Registration No. 6

1. Rock of ag - es, cleft for me, Let me hide my - self in Thee.
2. Not the la - bours of my hands, Can ful - fil Thy laws de-mands.

Let the wa - ter and the blood, From Thy riv - en side which flowed,
Could my zeal no res-pite know, Could my tears for ev - er flow,

Be of sin the dou - ble cure Cleanse me from its guilt and power.
All for sin could not a - tone, Thou must save and Thou a - lone.

3. Nothing in my hand I bring,
   Simply to Thy Cross I cling;
   Naked, come to Thee for dress:
   Helpless, look to Thee for grace;
   Foul, I to the fountain fly;
   Wash me, Saviour, or I die.

4. While I draw this fleeting breath,
   When mine eyes shall close in death,
   When I soar through tracts unknown,
   See Thee on Thy judgement throne,
   Rock of Ages, cleft for me,
   Let me hide myself in Thee.

"When I Survey The Wonderous Cross"

Registration No. 3

3. See from His head, His hands, His feet,
   Sorrow and love flow mingled down;
   Did e'er such love and sorrow meet,
   Or thorns compose so rich a Crown?

4. His dying crimson, like a robe,
   Spreads o'er His body on the Tree;
   Then am I dead to all the globe,
   And all the globe is dead to me.

5. Were the whole realm of nature mine,
   That were a present far too small;
   Love so amazing, so divine,
   Demands my soul, my life, my all.

"Stand Up, Stand Up For Jesus"

Registration No. 2

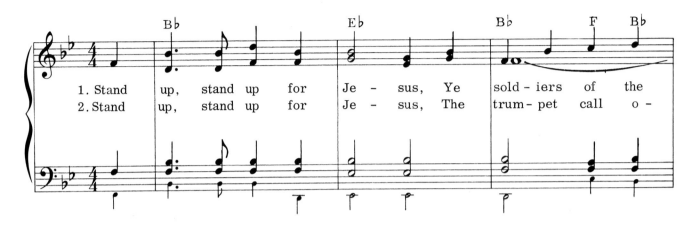

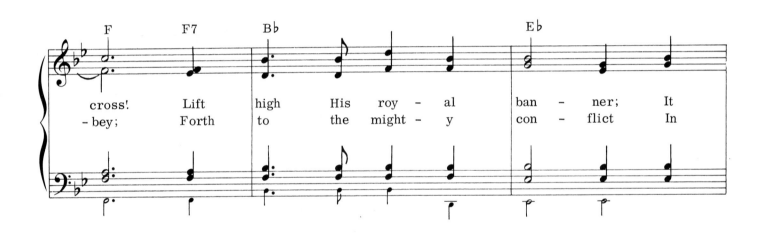

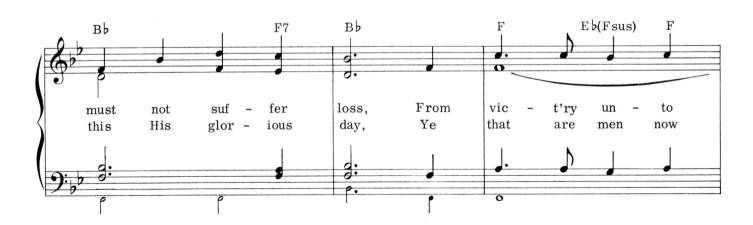

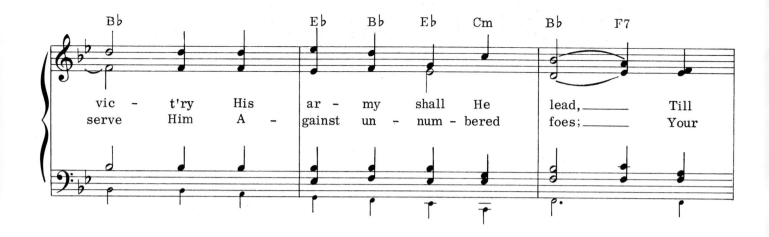

vic - t'ry His ar - my shall He lead,_____ Till
serve Him A - gainst un - num - bered foes;_____ Your

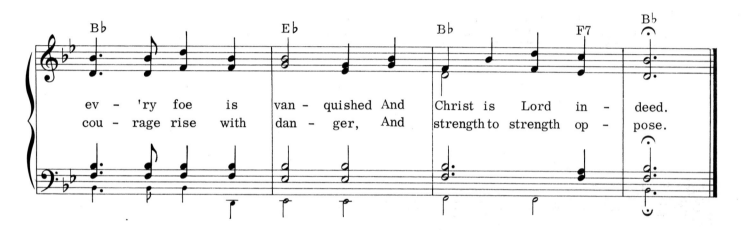

ev - 'ry foe is van - quished And Christ is Lord in - deed.
cou - rage rise with dan - ger, And strength to strength op - pose.

3. Stand up, stand up for Jesus!
   Stand in His strength alone;
   The arm of flesh will fail you,
   Ye dare not trust your own.
   Put on the gospel armour,
   Each piece put on with prayer:
   Where duty calls or danger,
   Be never wanting there.

4. Stand up, stand up for Jesus!
   Each soldier to his post;
   Close up the broken column
   And shout through all the host.
   Make good the loss so heavy
   In those that still remain;
   And prove to all around you
   That death itself is gain.

5. Stand up, stand up for Jesus!
   The strife will not be long;
   This day the noise of battle,
   The next the victor's song.
   To him that overcometh
   A crown of life shall be:
   He with the King of Glory
   Shall reign eternally.

"We Plough The Fields And Scatter"

Registration No. 5

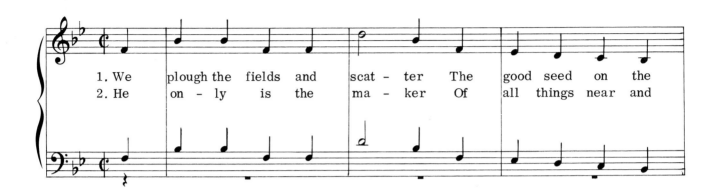

1. We plough the fields and scat - ter The good seed on the
2. He on - ly is the ma - ker Of all things near and

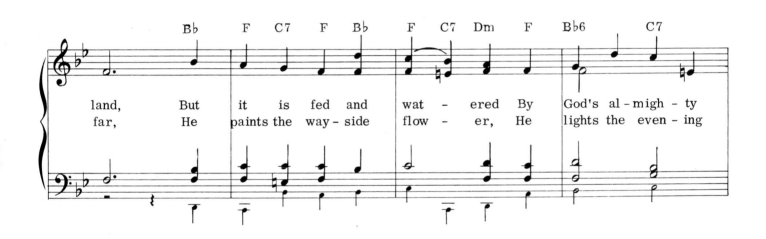

land, But it is fed and wat - ered By God's al - migh - ty
far, He paints the way - side flow - er, He lights the even - ing

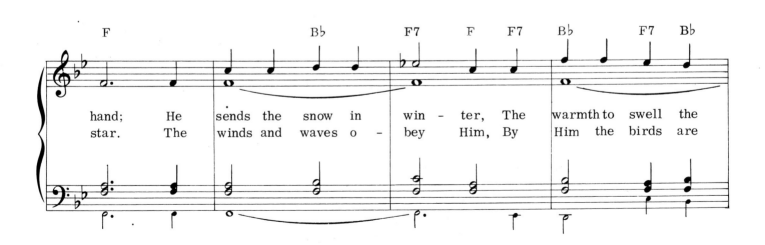

hand; He sends the snow in win - ter, The warmth to swell the
star. The winds and waves o - bey Him, By Him the birds are

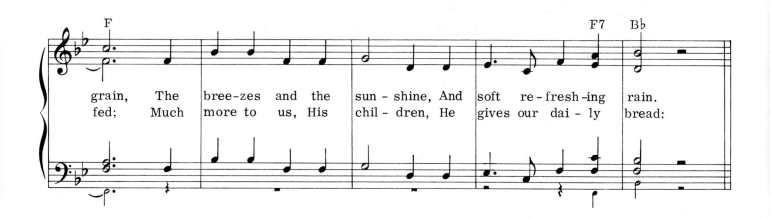

grain, The bree-zes and the sun - shine, And soft re-fresh-ing rain.
fed; Much more to us, His chil - dren, He gives our dai - ly bread:

Refrain

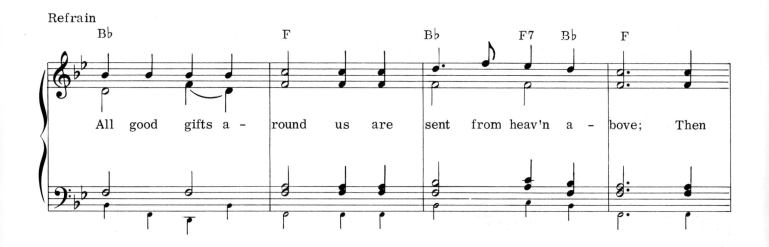

All good gifts a - round us are sent from heav'n a - bove; Then

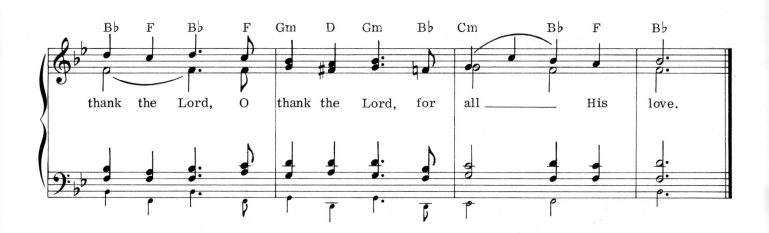

thank the Lord, O thank the Lord, for all _____ His love.

3. We thank Thee then, O Father,
   For all things bright and good;
   The seed-time and the harvest,
   Our life, our health, our food.
   No gifts have we to offer
   For all Thy love imparts,
   But that which Thou desirest,
   Our humble, thankful hearts.
   All good gifts etc.

"Each Step Of The Way"

Words & Music: Redd Harper

Registration No. 3

Just live for to - day. _____ I'm

fol - low - ing Jes - us _____ Each

Step Of The Way. _____

2. The pathway is narrow,
   But He leads me on.
   I walk in His shadow,
   My fears are all gone.
   My spirit grows stronger,
   Each moment each day,
   For Jesus is leading,
   Each Step Of The Way.

"Old Rugged Cross, (The)"

Registration No. 2

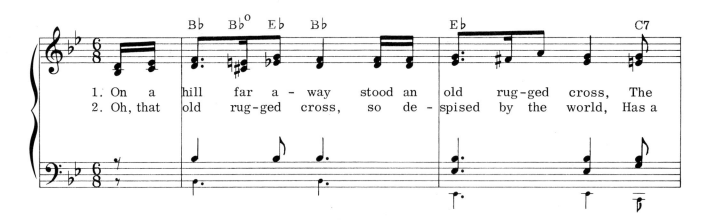

1. On a hill far a-way stood an old rug-ged cross, The
2. Oh, that old rug-ged cross, so de-spised by the world, Has a

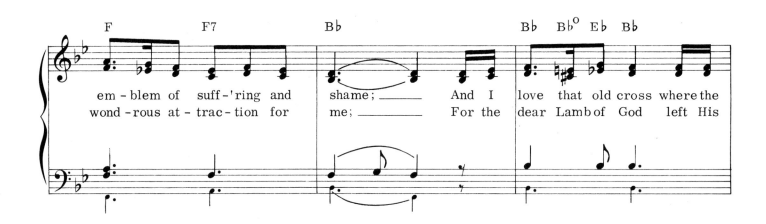

em-blem of suff-'ring and shame; And I love that old cross where the
wond-rous at-trac-tion for me; For the dear Lamb of God left His

dear-est and best For a world of lost sin-ners was slain. So I'll
glo-ry a-bove To bear it to dark Cal-va-ry. So I'll

Refrain

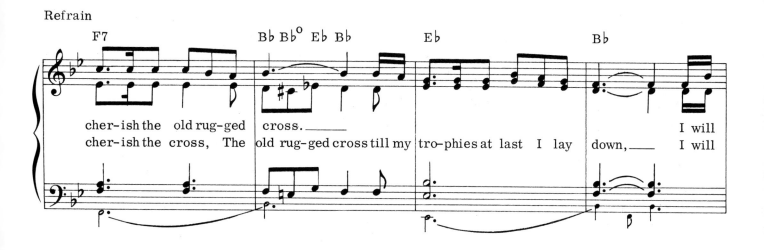

cher-ish the old rug-ged cross._____
cher-ish the cross, The old rug-ged cross till my tro-phies at last I lay down,_____ I will

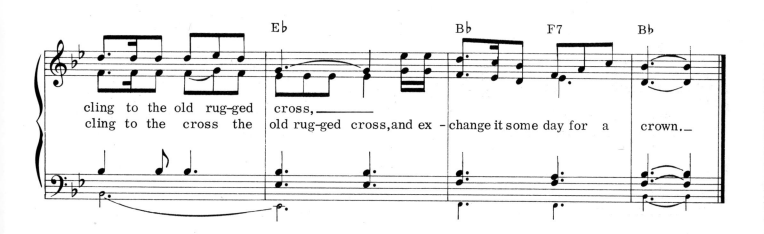

cling to the old rug-ged cross,_____
cling to the cross the old rug-ged cross, and ex-change it some day for a crown._

3. In the old rugged cross, stained with love so divine,
   A wondrous beauty I see;
   For 'twas on that old cross Jesus suffered and died
   To pardon and sanctify me.
       So I'll cherish etc.

4. To the old rugged cross, I will ever be true,
   Its shame and reproach gladly bear;
   Then He'll call me some day to my home far away,
   Where His glory for ever I'll share.
       So I'll cherish etc.

"All People That On Earth Do Dwell"

Registration No. 2

3. O enter then His gates with praise,
   Approach with joy His courts unto:
   Praise, laud, and bless His name always,
   For it is seemly so to do.

4. For why? the Lord our God is good;
   His mercy is for ever sure:
   His truth at all times firmly stood,
   And shall from age to age endure.

5. To Father, Son, and Holy Ghost,
   The God whom heaven and earth adore,
   From men and from the angel-host
   Be praise and glory evermore.

"Eternal Father, Strong To Save"

Registration No. 5

3. O sacred Spirit, who didst brood
   Upon the waters dark and rude,
   And bid their angry tumult cease,
   And give, for wild confusion, peace:
   O hear us when we cry to Thee
   For those in peril on the sea.

4. O Trinity of love and power,
   Our brethren shield in danger's hour;
   From rock and tempest, fire and foe,
   Protect them wheresoe'er they go;
   And ever let there rise to Thee
   Glad hymns of praise from land and sea.

"There Is A Green Hill Far Away"

Registration No. 3

3. He died that we might be forgiven,
He died to make us good;
That we might go at last to Heaven,
Saved by His precious blood.

4. There was no other good enough
To pay the price of sin;
He only could unlock the gate
Of Heaven, and let us in.

5. O dearly, dearly has He loved,
And we must love Him too,
And trust in His redeeming blood,
And try His works to do.

"Were You There?"

Arranged by: Stan Butcher

Registration No. 6

2. Were You There when they laid Him in the tomb?
   Were You There when they laid Him in the tomb?
   Oh, sometimes it causes me to tremble, tremble.
   Were You There when they laid Him in the tomb?

"Mine Eyes Have Seen The Glory"

Registration No. 5

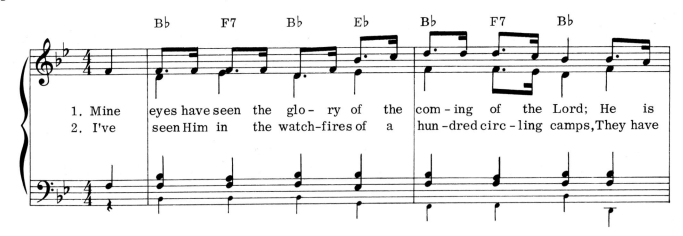

1. Mine eyes have seen the glo - ry of the com - ing of the Lord; He is
2. I've seen Him in the watch-fires of a hun - dred circ - ling camps, They have

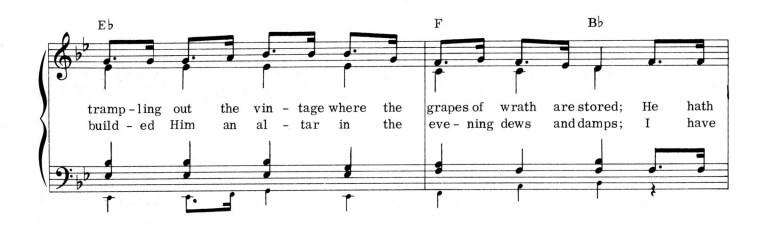

tramp - ling out the vin - tage where the grapes of wrath are stored; He hath
build - ed Him an al - tar in the eve - ning dews and damps; I have

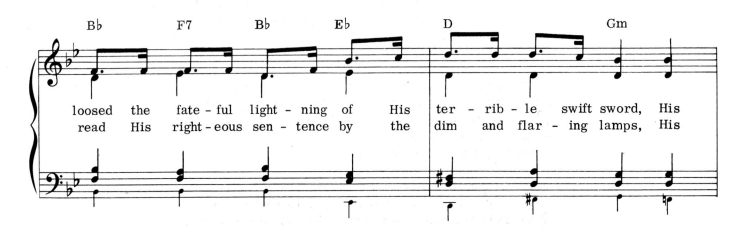

loosed the fate - ful light - ning of His ter - rib - le swift sword, His
read His right - eous sen - tence by the dim and flar - ing lamps, His

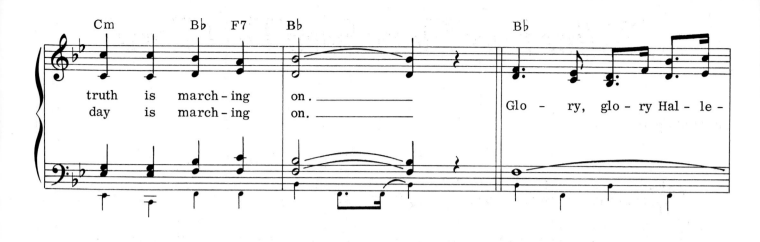

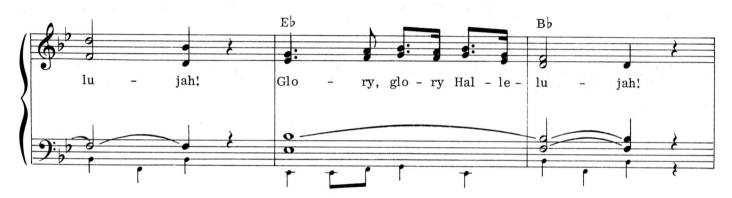

3. I have read a fiery gospel writ in burnished rows of steel,
   "As ye deal with My contemner, so with you My grace shall deal."
   Let the hero born of woman crush the serpent with His heel,
   Since God is marching on.
       Glory, glory, Hallelujah! etc.

4. He hath sounded forth the trumpet that shall never call retreat;
   He is sifting out the hearts of men before His judgement seat;
   O, be swift, my soul, to answer Him: be jubilant, my feet!
   Our God is marching on.
       Glory, glory, Hallelujah! etc.

5. In the beauty of the lilies Christ was born, across the sea,
   With a glory in His bosom that transfigures you and me;
   As He died to make men holy, let us live to make men free,
   While God is marching on.
       Glory, glory, Hallelujah! etc.

"Tell Me The Old, Old Story"

Registration No. 5

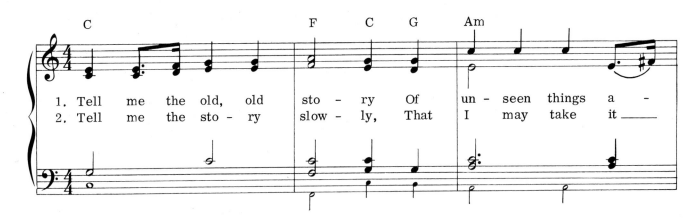

1. Tell me the old, old sto - ry Of un - seen things a -
2. Tell me the sto - ry slow - ly, That I may take it

- bove ___ Of Je - sus and ___ His ___ glo - ry, Of Je - sus ___ and His ___
in ___ That won - der - ful ___ re - demp - tion, God's rem - e - dy for ___

love, Tell ___ me the sto - ry simp - ly, As to ___ a ___ lit - tle
sin. Tell ___ me the sto - ry of - ten, For I ___ for - get so

child,   For   I am   weak and___   wea - ry,   And   help - less and   de - fil'd.
soon;   The   "early   dew" of ___   morn - ing   Has   passed a - way   at ___ noon.

Refrain

Tell   me   the old, old   sto - ry,   Tell   me   the old, old   sto - ry,

Tell   me   the old, old   sto - ry,   of   Je - sus   and ___   His   love.

3. Tell me the story softly,
    With earnest tones and grave;
    Remember, I'm the sinner
    Whom Jesus came to save.
    Tell me the story always,
    If you would really be,
    In any time of trouble
    A comforter to me.
    Tell me the old, old story etc.

4. Tell me the same old story,
    When you have cause to fear,
    That this world's empty glory
    Is costing me too dear:
    Yes, and when that world's glory
    Is dawning on my soul,
    Tell me the old, old story:
    "Christ Jesus makes thee whole."
    Tell me the old, old story etc.

"Jerusalem The Golden"

Registration No. 4

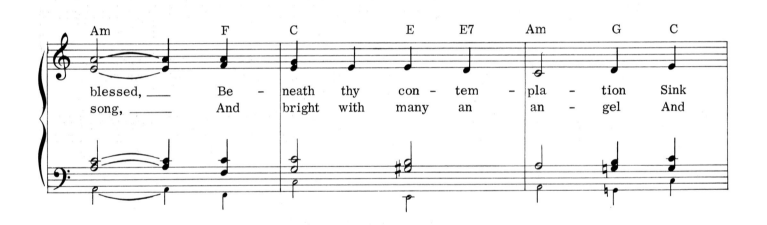

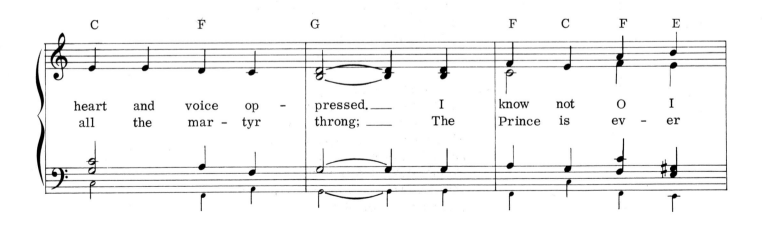

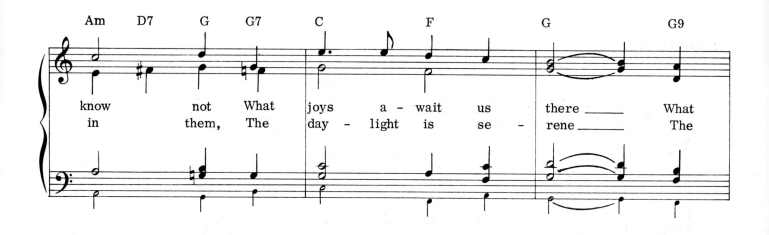

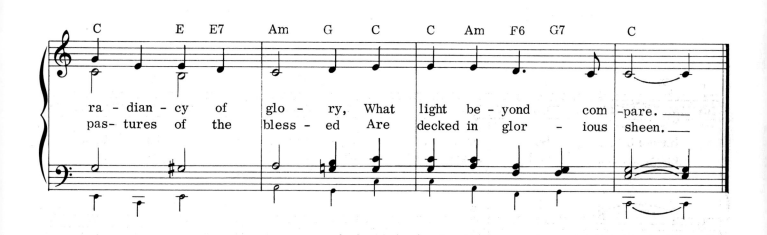

3. There is the throne of David,
   And there from care released,
   The shout of them that triumph,
   The song of them that feast;
   And they who, with their Leader,
   Have conquered in the fight,
   For ever and for ever
   Are clad in robes of white.

4. Jerusalem the glorious,
   The home of God's elect;
   O dear and future vision
   That eager hearts expect!
   Jesu, in mercy bring us
   To that dear land of rest,
   Who art, with God the Father,
   And Spirit, ever blest.

"He Who Would Valiant Be"

Registration No. 4

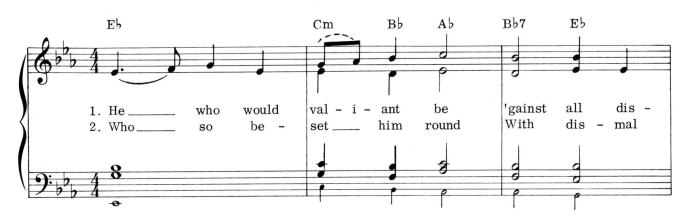

1. He _____ who would val - i - ant be 'gainst all dis -
2. Who _____ so be - set _____ him round With dis - mal

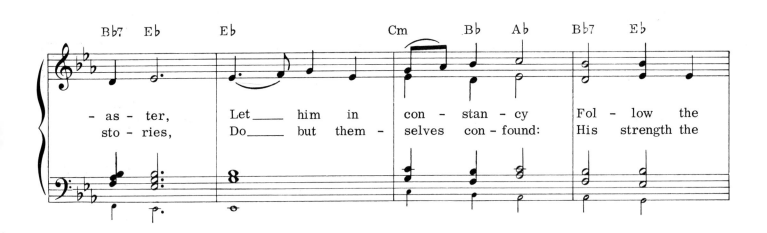

- as - ter,   Let _____ him in con - stan - cy Fol - low the
sto - ries,   Do _____ but them - selves con - found: His strength the

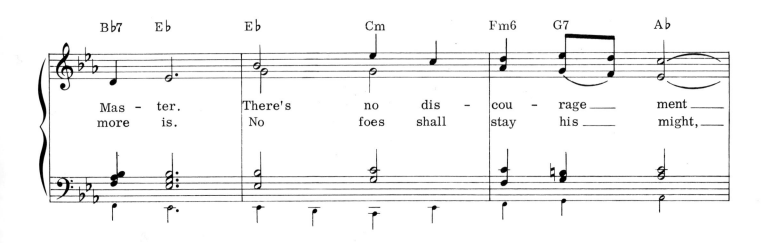

Mas - ter. There's no dis - cou - rage _____ ment _____
more is. No foes shall stay his _____ might, _____

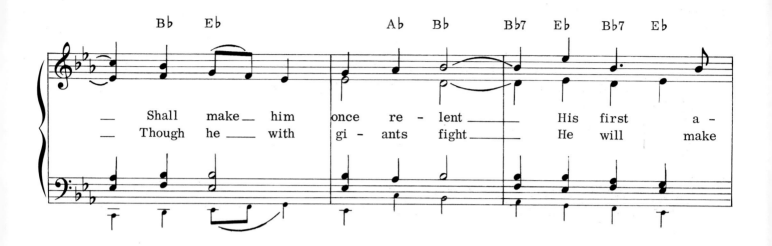

Shall make him once re - lent   His first   a -
Though he   with gi - ants fight   He will   make

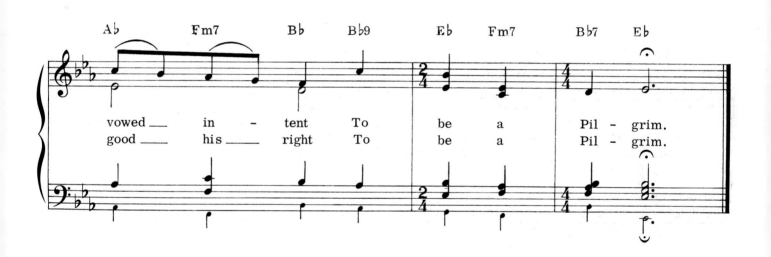

vowed   in - tent To   be   a   Pil - grim.
good   his   right To   be   a   Pil - grim.

3. Since, Lord, Thou dost defend
   Us with Thy Spirit,
   We know we at the end
   Shall life inherit.
   Then fancies flee away!
   I'll fear not what men say,
   I'll labour night and day
   To be a Pilgrim.

"Holy, Holy, Holy"

Registration No. 6

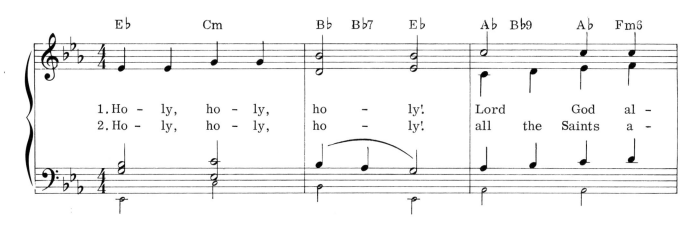

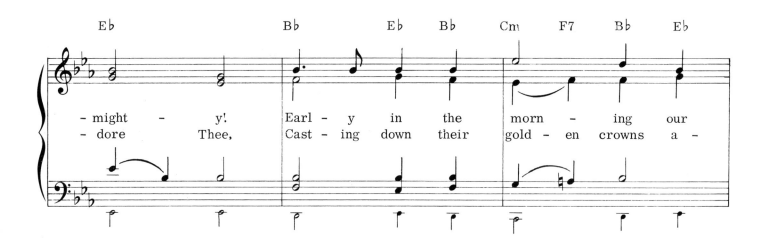

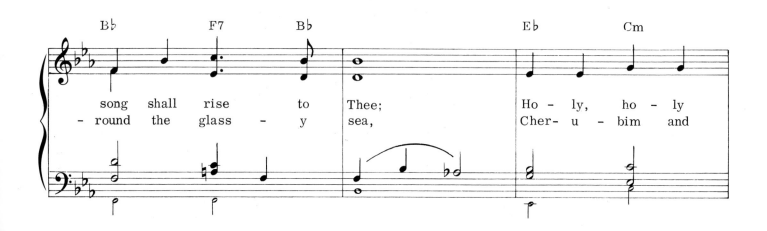

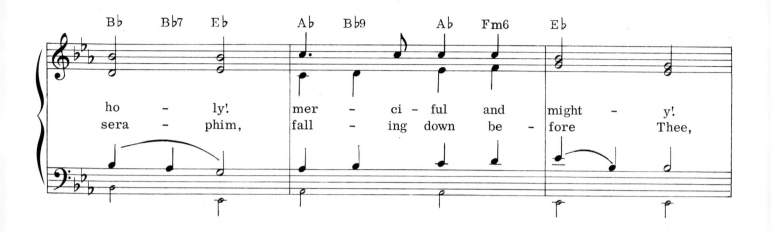

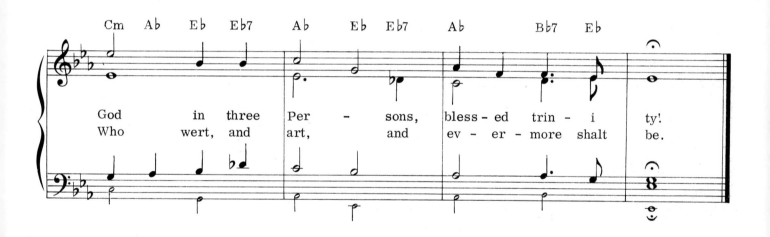

3. Holy, holy, holy! though the darkness hide Thee,
   Though the eye of sinful man Thy glory may not see,
   Only Thou art holy, there is none beside Thee
   Perfect in power, in love and purity.

4. Holy, holy, holy! Lord God Almighty!
   All Thy works shall praise Thy name, in earth and sky and sea:
   Holy, holy, holy! merciful and mighty!
   God in three Persons, blessed trinity.

"All Things Bright And Beautiful"

Registration No. 2

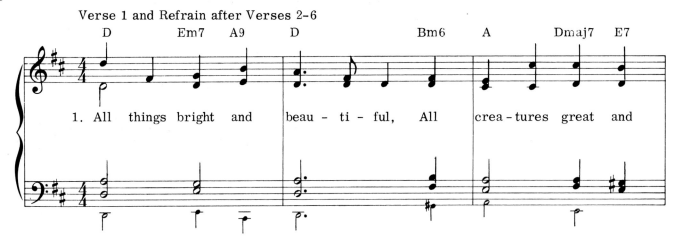

Verse 1 and Refrain after Verses 2-6

1. All things bright and beau-ti-ful, All crea-tures great and

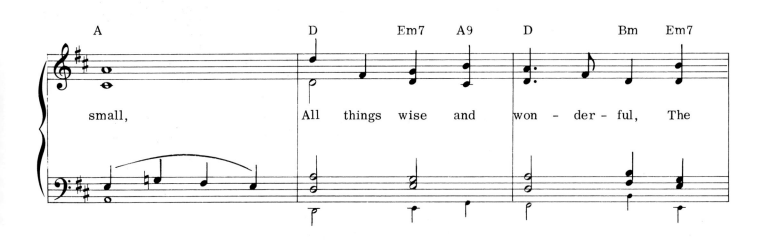

small, All things wise and won-der-ful, The

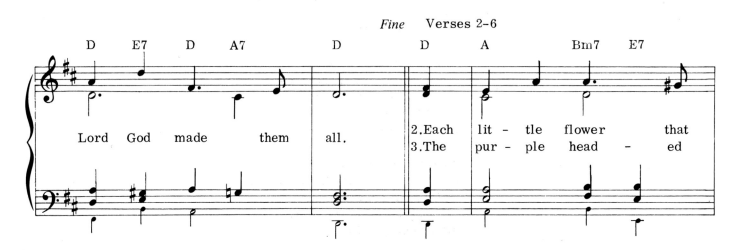

Fine Verses 2-6

Lord God made them all.

2.Each lit-tle flower that
3.The pur-ple head-ed

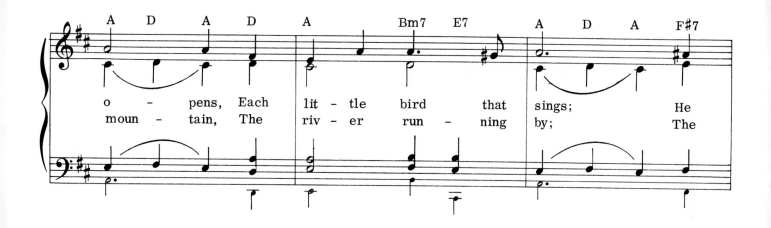

o - pens, Each lit - tle bird that sings; He
moun - tain, The riv - er run - ning by; The

D.C. al FINE

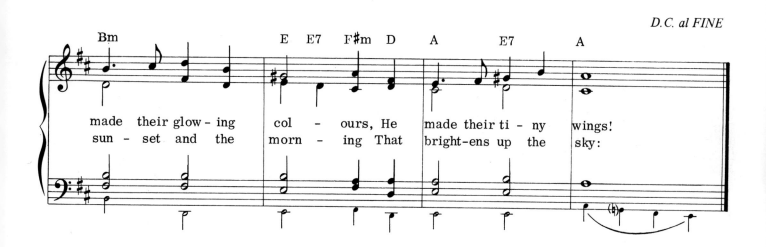

made their glow - ing col - ours, He made their ti - ny wings!
sun - set and the morn - ing That bright-ens up the sky:

4. The cold wind in the winter,
   The pleasant summer sun,
   The ripe fruits in the garden,
   He made them ev'ry one:
   All things bright etc.

5. The tall trees in the greenwood,
   The meadows where we play,
   The rushes by the water
   We gather ev'ry day:
   All things bright etc.

6. He gave us eyes to see them,
   And lips that we might tell
   How great is God Almighty,
   Who has made all things well:
   All things bright etc.

29

"Praise My Soul The King Of Heaven"

Registration No. 5

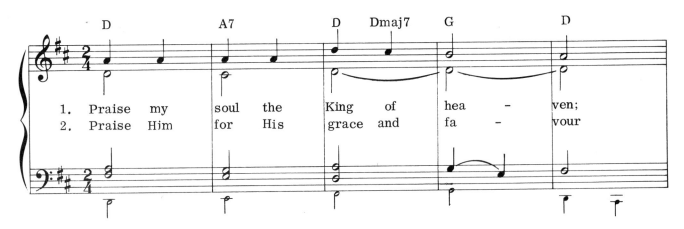

1. Praise my soul the King of hea - ven;
2. Praise Him for His grace and fa - vour

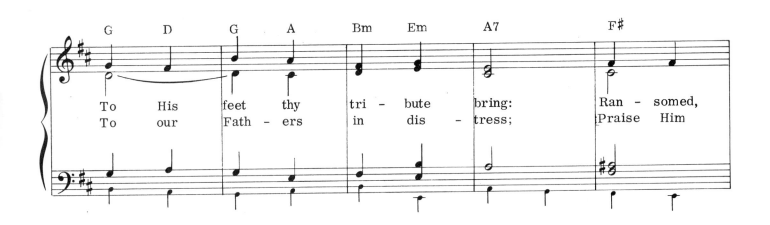

To His feet thy tri - bute bring: Ran - somed,
To our Fath - ers in dis - tress; Praise Him

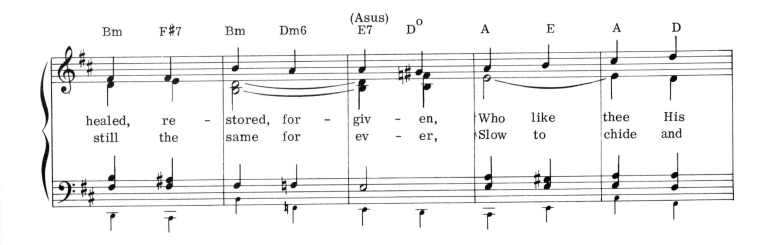

healed, re - stored, for - giv - en, Who like thee His
still the same for ev - er, Slow to chide and

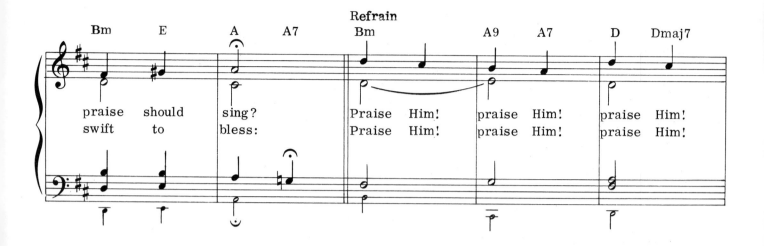

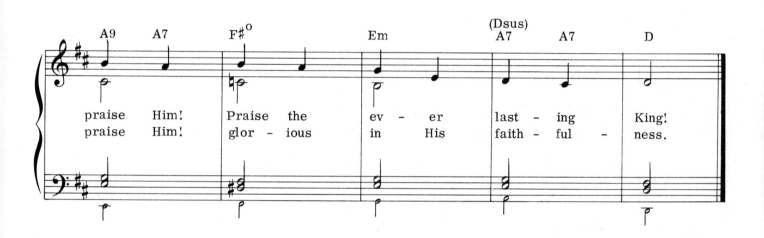

3. Father-like He tends and spares us;
   Well our feeble frame He knows;
   In His hands He gently bears us,
   Rescues us from all our foes:
   Praise Him!, praise Him!,
   Praise Him!, praise Him!,
   Widely as His mercy flows!

4. Frail as summer's flower we flourish,
   Blows the wind and it is gone;
   But while mortals rise and perish
   God endures unchanging on.
   Praise Him! praise Him!
   Praise Him! praise Him!
   Praise the High Eternal One.

5. Angels, help us to adore Him,
   Ye behold Him face to face;
   Sun and moon, bow down before Him,
   Dwellers all in time and space:
   Praise Him! praise Him!
   Praise Him! praise Him!
   Praise with us the God of grace!

"Lonesome Road"

Words: Gene Austin.
Music: Nathaniel Shilkret

Registration No. 4

Look down, look down, That Lonesome road, ___ Be - fore you trav - el on. Look

up, look up, and see yo' mak-er, 'Fore Gabri - el blows his horn

Wear - y to-tin' such a load. Tredg-in' down that Lone-some road. Look

down, look down, that Lone-some road, ___ Be - fore you trav - el on. ___

2. True love, true love, what have I done,
That you should treat me so?
You caused me to walk and talk,
Like I never did before.

Weary totin' such a load,
Tredging down that Lonesome Road.

Look down, look down,
That Lonesome Road,
Before you travel on.

"Jesus Is Kind"

By: Lindy Janes

Registration No. 7

2. When doubt and sorrow hover near,
Only believe and have no fear.
He is the light, the way you'll find,
Your answer there,
For He is kind.

"Church's One Foundation, (The)"

Registration No. 2

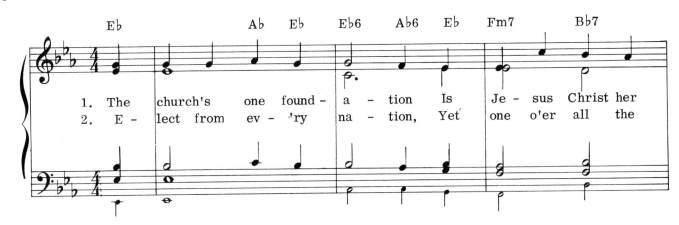

1. The church's one found - a - tion Is Je - sus Christ her
2. E - lect from ev - 'ry na - tion, Yet one o'er all the

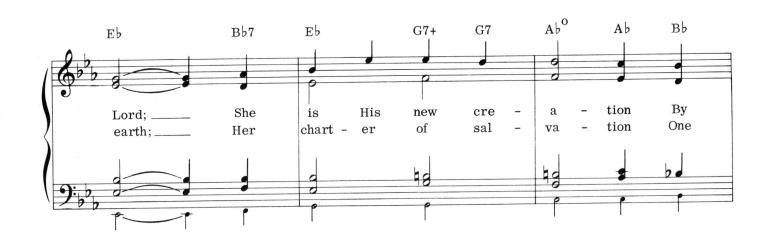

Lord; ___ She is His new cre - a - tion By
earth; ___ Her chart - er of sal - va - tion One

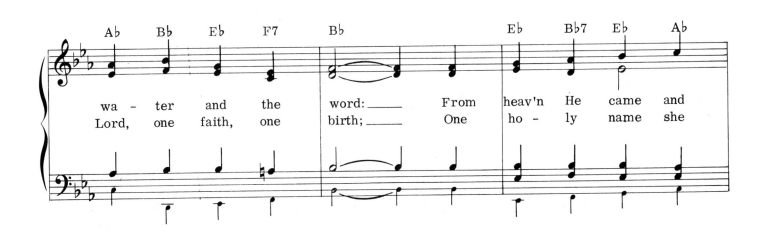

wa - ter and the word: ___ From heav'n He came and
Lord, one faith, one birth; ___ One ho - ly name she

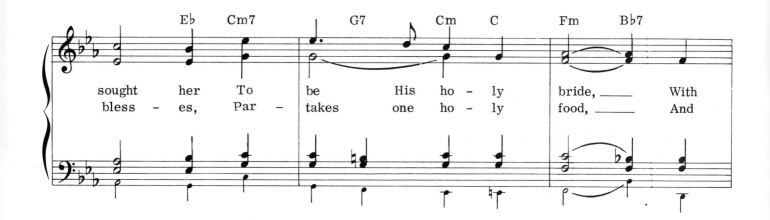

3. Though with a scornful wonder
   Men see her sore oppressed,
   By schisms rent asunder,
   By heresies distressed,
   Yet saints their watch are keeping,
   Their cry goes up, "How long?"
   And soon the night of weeping
   Shall be the morn of song.

4. 'Mid toil and tribulation,
   And tumult of her war,
   She waits the consummation
   Of peace for evermore;
   Till with the vision glorious
   Her longing eyes are blest,
   And the great Church victorious
   Shall be the Church at rest.

5. Yet she on earth hath union
   With God the Three in One
   And mystic sweet communion
   With those whose rest is won:
   O happy ones and holy!
   Lord give us grace that we
   Like them, the meek and lowly,
   On high may dwell with Thee.

"O Worship The King"

Registration No. 3

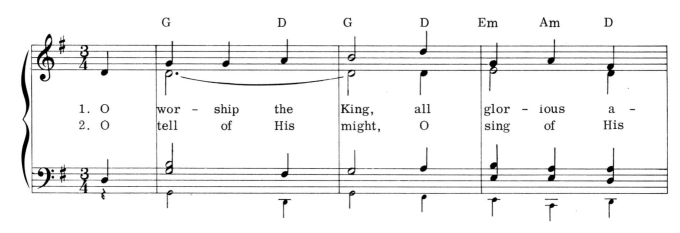

1. O wor - ship the King, all glor - ious a -
2. O tell of the His might, O sing of His

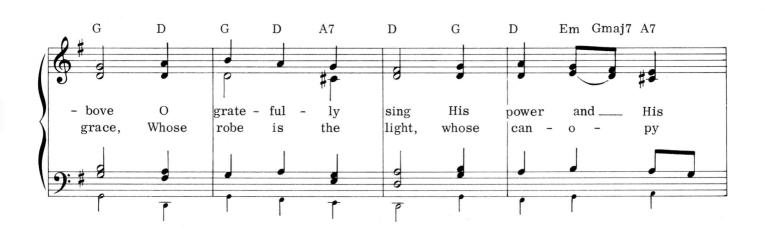

- bove O grate - ful - ly sing His power and ___ His
grace, Whose robe is the light, whose can - o - py

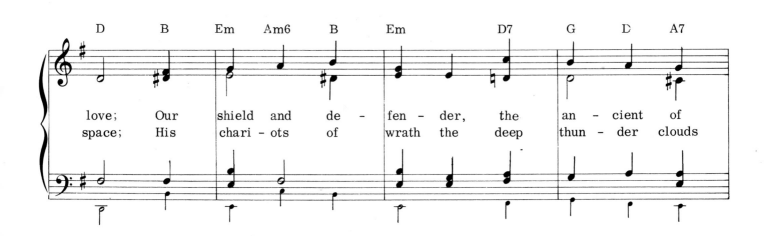

love; Our shield and de - fen - der, the an - cient of
space; His chari - ots of wrath the deep thun - der clouds

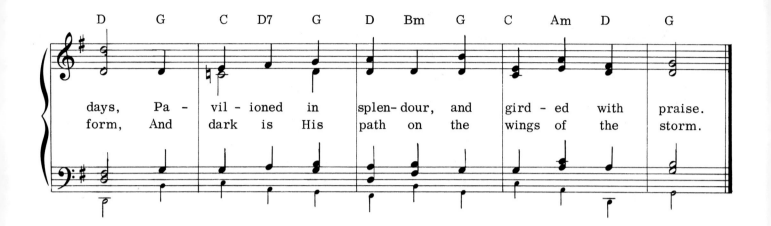

days, Pa - vil - ioned in splen- dour, and gird - ed with praise.
form, And dark is His path on the wings of the storm.

3. The earth with its store of wonders untold,
   Almighty, Thy power hath founded of old;
   Hath 'stablished it fast by a changeless decree,
   And round it hath cast, like a mantle, the sea.

4. Thy bountiful care what tongue can recite?
   It breathes in the air, it shines in the light;
   It streams from the hills, it descends to the plain,
   And sweetly distils in the dew and the rain.

5. Frail children of dust, and feeble as frail,
   In Thee do we trust, nor find Thee to fail;
   Thy mercies how tender, how firm to the end,
   Our Maker, Defender, Redeemer and Friend.

6. O measureless Might, ineffable Love,
   While angels delight to hymn Thee above.
   Thy humbler creation, though feeble their lays,
   With true adoration shall sing to Thy praise.

"Lord My Shepherd, (The)"

Registration No. 7

1. The Lord's my shepherd, I'll not want, He makes me down to lie In pastures green; He leadeth me The quiet waters by.

2. My soul He doth restore again, And me to walk doth make With-in the paths of righteousness, E'en for His own name's sake.

3. Yea, though I walk in death's dark vale,
   Yet will I fear none ill;
   For Thou art with me, and Thy rod
   And staff me comfort still.

4. My table Thou hast furnished
   In presence of my foes;
   My head Thou dost with oil anoint,
   And my cup overflows.

5. Goodness and mercy all my life
   Shall surely follow me;
   And in God's house for evermore
   My dwelling-place shall be.

"Lead Us Heavenly Father"

Registration No. 4

3. Spirit of our God, descending,
   Fill our hearts with heavenly joy,
   Love with ev'ry passion blending,
   Pleasure that can never cloy:
   Thus provided, pardoned, guided,
   Nothing can our peace destroy.

"How Great Thou Art"

Registration No. 5

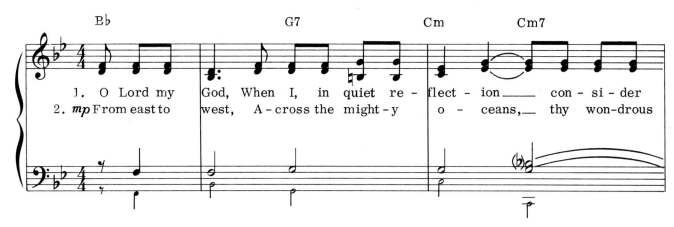

fills with glow-ing love for Thee How great Thou art! ____ How great Thou art! Then my heart

fills with glow-ing love for Thee, How great Thou art! ____ how great Thou art! ____

3. And when I think of mankind frail and feeble,
    Without hope and desolate within;
    Then Jesus came to rescue us from danger,
    When on the cross He saved us all from sin.
        Then my heart fills etc.

"Through The Night Of Doubt And Sorrow"

Registration No. 7

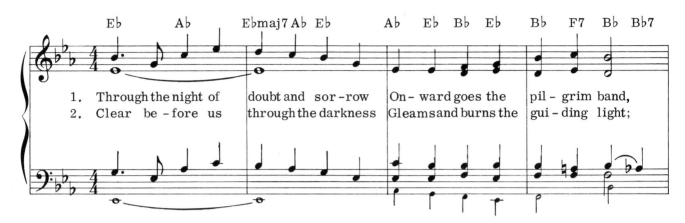

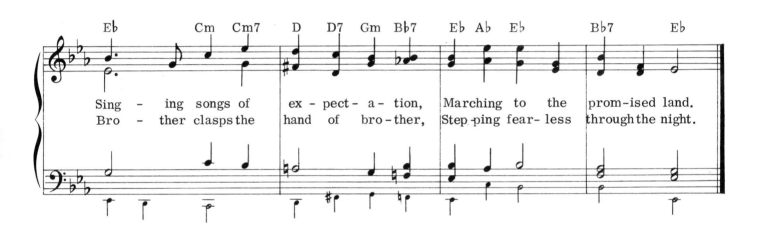

3. One the light of God's own Presence
   O'er His ransomed people shed,
   Chasing far the gloom and terror,
   Brightening all the path we tread.

4. One the object of our journey,
   One the faith which never tires,
   One the earnest looking forward,
   One the hope our God inspires.

5. One the strain that lips of thousands
   Lift as from the heart of one;
   One the conflict, one the peril,
   One the march in God begun:

6. One the gladness of rejoicing
   On the far eternal shore,
   Where the One Almighty Father
   Reigns in love for evermore.

7. Onward, therefore, pilgrim brothers,
   Onward with the Cross our aid;
   Bear its shame and fight its battle,
   Till we rest beneath its shade.

8. Soon shall come the great awaking,
   Soon the rending of the tomb;
   Then the scattering of all shadows,
   And the end of toil and gloom.

Organ Registration Page.

Registration No.	*Single-Manual Organs	*All Electronic Organs		*All Drawbar Organs	
1	8' 4' I II III	Upper: Lower: Pedal:	Flute 8' Melodia 8' 8', Soft	Upper: Lower: Pedal:	60 8808 000 (00) 5554 433 (1) 4-2 (Spinet 3)
2	8' I II	Upper: Lower: Pedal:	Cello 16', Trumpet 8', Flute 8', 4' Reed 8', Viola 8' (String 8') 16', 8', Full	Upper: Lower: Pedal:	40 8606 005 (00) 4543 222 (1) 4-2 (Spinet 3)
3	8' 2' I III V	Upper: Lower: Pedal:	Flute 16', (Tibia 16'), Clarinet 8', (Reed 8') Diapason 8' 16', Soft	Upper: Lower: Pedal:	60 8805 005 (00) 5544 321 (0) 4-2 (Spinet 3)
4	8' 4' 2' I II III V	Upper: Lower: Pedal:	Flute 16', (Tibia 16'), Flute 8' Diapason 8', Melodia 8' 16', 8' Medium	Upper: Lower: Pedal:	80 8080 800 (00) 6544 444 (2) 4-2 (Spinet 3)
5	8' 4' II	Upper: Lower: Pedal:	Flute 16', (Tibia 16'), Flute 8', Reed 8', Horn 8' Melodia 8', Diapason 8' 16', 8' Full	Upper: Lower: Pedal:	50 8806 006 (00) 5555 443 (3) 4-2 (Spinet 3)
6	8' 4' 2' I II V	Upper: Lower: Pedal:	Flute 16', (Tibia 16'), Flute 8', 4' Diapason 8', Horn 8' 16', 8' Medium	Upper: Lower: Pedal:	00 8080 600 (00) 4433 222 (0) 4-2 (Spinet 3)
7	8' II IV V	Upper: Lower: Pedal:	Diapason 8' Flute 8' 8' Medium	Upper: Lower: Pedal:	60 8008 000 (00) 5544 000 (0) 4-2 (Spinet 3)

* Vibrato and Reverberation left to personal preference

Printed by J B Offset (Marks Tey) Limited, Marks Tey, Colchester, Essex.